Please return/renew this item by the last date shown

worcestershire
countycouncil
Cultural Services

# WATERWAYS

Images From An Industrial Past

## British Waterways – 2,000 miles of history

British Waterways runs the country's two-centuries-old working heritage of canals and river navigations. It conserves the historic buildings, structures and landscapes which blend to create the unique environment of the inland waterways, and protects their valuable and varied habitats.

As part of its commitment to the heritage of the waterways, British Waterways was instrumental in setting up The Waterways Trust, which aims to educate the public about the inland waterways and to promote the restoration and preservation of their rich architectural, historical and environmental heritage.

The Waterways Trust is a partnership between British Waterways, The National Waterways Museum at Gloucester, the Boat Museum at Ellesmere Port and the Canal Museum, Stoke Bruerne. The Trust cares for the National Waterways Collection, the country's pre-eminent collection of canal artefacts, documents and boats which are on view to the public at all the museums.

The Waterways Trust also manages the British Waterways Archive, a unique collection of inland waterway records dating back to the late seventeenth century and containing the largest documentary and photographic resource of its kind in Britain. Supported by the Heritage Lottery Fund, the archive is the subject of an ambitious project to make the collection available to all via the Internet. The new Cyber Archive will, for the first time, create a single catalogue of Britain's canal archives, revolutionizing research into the history of the inland waterways.

For more information about British Waterways call 01923 201120 or visit the website at www.britishwaterways.co.uk.

For access to the archive, or to get up-to-date information about the Cyber Archive project, call 01452 318041.

# WATERWAYS
## Images From An Industrial Past

*Nick Billingham*

*in association with British Waterways*

*To all the people shown in these photographs
in thanks for their part in keeping the canal system alive.
Anonymous now, and enduring much poverty during their working lives,
without them the canals would be nothing more
than a footnote in history books.*

TEMPUS

First published 1999

PUBLISHED IN THE UNITED KINGDOM BY:

Tempus Publishing Ltd
The Mill, Brimscombe Port
Stroud, Gloucestershire GL5 2QG

PUBLISHED IN THE UNITED STATES OF AMERICA BY

Tempus Publishing Inc.
2 Cumberland Street
Charleston, SC 29401

Tempus books are available in France, Germany and Belgium
from the following addresses:

| Tempus Publishing Group | Tempus Publishing Group | Tempus Publishing Group |
|---|---|---|
| 21 Avenue de la République | Gustav-Adolf-Straße 3 | Place de L'Alma 4/5 |
| 37300 Joué-lès-Tours | 99084 Erfurt | 1200 Brussels |
| FRANCE | GERMANY | BELGIUM |

British Library Cataloguing in Publication Data.
A catalogue record for this book is available from the British Library.

ISBN 0 7524 1725 8

Typesetting and origination by Tempus Publishing.
PRINTED AND BOUND IN GREAT BRITAIN.

# Contents

The Birmingham day boats shifted millions of tons of coal every year. Here at Hednesford they were loaded directly from narrow-gauge coal trucks. The boats were treated rather like industrial-sized wheel barrows and would be expected to last no more than ten years. Mostly they were made from pitch pine, and when the bottom was worn out they were hauled onto the bank and converted into firewood. Of the thousands that were made less than a couple of dozen survive.

# Sources

Many thanks are due to British Waterways Archives, Walsall Local History Centre and the Shakespeare Birthplace Trust for the use of these photographs.

# Introduction

Hidden away behind city streets or meandering through fields, our canals and waterways have a secret charm. Life takes a slower pace on the water and the people you meet are more relaxed. Buried deep within the heart of the twentieth century, with all its frenetic speed and glitzy chrome, is the cut, a gentle lapping of water against ancient brickwork. The network of waterways stretches green fingers of tranquillity deep into the concrete heart of cities, it brings life and colour to the countryside and above all it maintains a strong physical link with our heritage. It's the kind of link that you can get to grips with: blue bricks, blue steel and engines that run at the same speed as your heart.

The canal system was constructed at the end of the eighteenth century. The impetus for its construction was at first largely driven by one man, the famous Duke of Bridgewater. As a young man he had seen the extensive canal system at work on the continent, so he applied this technology to improving his mines at Worsley, near Manchester. Although his ideas were ridiculed at first, once his Bridgewater Canal opened it became obvious that a canal was infinitely better than the crude river navigations already in existence. The duke had sacrificed much of his wealth in the project and was even known to throw off his coat and work alongside the men, but the rewards he reaped once his cut opened in 1761 provided inspiration for a new generation of canal entrepreneurs.

The chief engineer of the duke's Bridgewater Canal was James Brindley, who was soon in demand by several other canal ventures. He had a personal dream of a 'Grand Cross' of waterways linking all England's large river navigations. Canals linking the Trent and Mersey and southwards through the industrial Midlands to the Thames and Severn all looked to him for engineering experience. It was here, in the 1770s, that the idea of a standard 'narrow' boat some 7ft wide and 70ft long became the accepted norm for inland waterway boats. Although they may look small to our modern eyes, they carried a much greater load than most of the shallow-draught, wide-beamed riverboats of the day. One boat could carry 25 tons, at a time when the only competing transport was a wagon on unmetalled roads. Entrepreneurs like Josiah Wedgewood backed the new schemes wholeheartedly.

Wedgewood had a particularly compelling interest in water transport, since the breakage rate of pottery transported by road was simply staggering and sometimes over half of his valuable plates would be smashed before arriving at their destination. Smooth and steady water transport was a distinct improvement. Coincidentally, Josiah Wedgewood's son, Thomas, used to experiment with an early form of photography, the silhouette. This primitive form of photography involved capturing the outline of a face on a plate coated with silver nitrate. It had been known for many years that some silver compounds were light sensitive, but this technique was one of the first to exploit this effect. The main drawback was that there was no way to fix the image, and it would gradually fade when exposed to light. It was to be a few more years before Thomas Wedgewood or anyone else could photograph the canals his father was constructing.

By the early 1770s canals such as the Trent and Mersey, the Staffordshire and Worcestershire and the Oxford Canal had been given the necessary approval by Parliament. In those days compulsory purchase of land was a very rare event. The Duke of Bridgewater had fought a long and hard battle to prove their value, but nevertheless digging a new canal was fraught with legal as well as physical problems. Simply getting the required Act of Parliament was a new and virtually unknown process. The aftermath of the South Sea Bubble, an unregulated investment scheme of the 1720s, was stringent regulation of any company wishing to raise capital by selling shares – it took an Act of Parliament to start a large company. Once the Act was obtained and the digging could commence, the problems of design and construction arose. Brindley advocated the use of 'contour' canals, arguing that it was cheaper to follow a particular contour around a hill or valley rather than plough straight through with a cutting or embankment. These early canals relied on a cheap construction method and even cheaper labour. Mostly they were dug during the winter months by local farm labourers who could be spared from the land. Brick kilns were erected close to the places where the bricks were needed and stone quarries opened to service the needs of the masons. The result was that each canal has a unique blend of

A modern photograph showing how simple and elegant some canal structures are. This is a lift bridge on the Trent and Mersey canal. The bridge deck is balanced by the arms and can be raised easily to let a boat pass.

Legging a boat through a tunnel was gruelling work. Here at Crick tunnel the boat finally emerges into the daylight to meet up with its horse, which has walked over the hill. Until the introduction of motorized tunnel tugs there were often teams of professional 'leggers' offering to do the work for a fee. It was probably the most hazardous occupation on the whole canal network.

materials: red brick where there was plenty of clay, limestone or granite if there was a quarry nearby. Canal architecture became vernacular in the extreme.

These first canals opened during the 1780s and proved to be highly profitable. The capital required for their construction was comparatively small since their routes, being primarily along land contours, required little in the way of expensive engineering works. The traffic multiplied: coal for London, wheat for Birmingham, and people everywhere. A couple of days on a boat were far more comfortable than a week on a stagecoach and passenger and parcel services bloomed. Heavy freight such as coal and iron began to drop in price. Coal in particular halved in price in the towns served by a canal. This was a boon to ordinary people, many of whom had previously relied on wood gathered from fast disappearing common land.

The financial and social benefit of the canals was proved, and the number of canals proposed doubled every year. No longer were they designed simply to link river navigations; they were proposed to serve towns, cities, coal fields and foundries. A network of waterways was being created that would serve most of the country. Unlike our modern network of motorways, however, each canal developed its own architecture from the ideas of its engineer, constrained by the materials he had at hand.

International events had their effect on this blooming transport system, with revolution and war in France galvanizing the British into action as they prepared to withstand invasion and support the monarchy. The government abandoned the gold standard in order to free vast amounts of capital into circulation. Proposals for canals peaked in 1793 when capital was available in huge quantities and enthusiasm was at a peak. It was clear that a system to transport not only peacetime products but also munitions was vital to the defence of the realm. Behind almost every scheme stood the Duke of Bridgewater, by now wealthy beyond the dreams of avarice. He was a solitary man, wrapped up in his vast estates, his only hobby collecting paintings, but he lent his support to canals whenever it was needed.

As the nineteenth century dawned, Europe was racked by war. In order to defeat the expansionist policies of revolutionary France the English government became desperate for money. Investing in canals became a lot less profitable than State Bonds; the new income tax didn't help matters either. The fledgling canal companies born in the years of 'Canal Mania' around 1793 became entangled in lengthy disputes with shareholders unwilling to invest further. This was a serious handicap to the companies, but a worse one soon emerged: the war was removing all the surplus labour from the land to the army. The ordinary English canal labourers, known as 'navvies' (from 'navigator') were off at war. They were replaced with itinerant labourers, often from Ireland. The navvies soon acquired a fearsome reputation for hard work and hard play. Villages along the route of the canals' construction were terrorised. Occasionally the local militia even had to be called to suppress riots. The navvies soon realised that they could virtually command their own price and the labour cost of digging the canals soared.

The war caused yet another headache for the new canal companies as the government had managed to set the respective values of gold, silver and copper coins out of all proportion to the value of the metals on the international markets. The value of copper in particular rose as it was needed for the manufacture of weapons. Small denomination coins like pennies vanished from circulation and the canal companies were forced to issue their own tokens to pay their staff. Tokens were redeemable at a company shop, but that soon led to accusations that the shop prices were inflated.

It may seem odd that the canals were completed at all. Nevertheless the demand for cheaper transport was so great that all the problems were overcome one way or another. New techniques such as 'cut and fill' were being tried so that the overall cost and length of the canal could be reduced. Huge aqueducts and tunnels were proposed to cut the cost of each endeavour. This was the birth of civil engineering as we know it today – and mostly by trial and error.

Most of the canals proposed in the 1790s were completed around 1815, usually costing twice the original estimate and ten years late (thus bearing an uncanny resemblance to modern civil engineering!). A few fell by the wayside, however.

Boats required fenders to prevent them and the lock gates breaking each other. Each fender is a woven web of rope around a core. It takes a great deal of skill and strength to make them.

Boats come in all shapes and sizes.

The Leominster canal, supposed to be 36 miles long, only had 18 miles built before everyone lost interest. Unfortunately for the shareholders, it was the middle 18 miles and was never connected to the rest of the system.

The vast majority of the canal system was complete by the end of the Napoleonic Wars, just in time to face a massive recession caused by the reintroduction of the gold standard and thousands of returning troops looking for work. It transpired that nearly half the paper money in circulation was either forged or backed by bankrupt provincial banks. In spite of this, the companies managed to survive and some even prospered although many of the more speculative ventures had a hard time of it indeed. This resulted in a severe shortage of investment in new routes and modernization. Carriers protested about delays and costs but there was little improvement. A constant source of complaint was the contour canals. Tolls were charged by the ton/mile, i.e. so many pence per ton per mile along the canal. A couple of pennies per ton soon added up. A good example of this would be Wormlieghton on the Oxford Canal. Two pence per ton per mile, or 40d per boat per mile, soon became 200d for the five miles that the canal route took to cover one mile as the crow flies. The boatmen soon worked out that the contour route cost 160d more than the cut-and-fill straight route. A week's wages for a labourer was around 60d (five shillings or 25p in modern money), which left the contour canals looking as though they were overcharging by the equivalent of hundreds of pounds in today's values.

It is hardly surprising that behind the scenes a new form of transport was being conceived. In the autumn of 1802 the railway visionary William James had tried to convince the Duke of Bridgewater to invest in railroads, with no success at all. The duke died the following spring leaving the canal system fatherless. In 1804 Richard Trevithick demonstrated the world's first true locomotive at the Pen-y-darren mine. William James was there, as well as other canal engineers like John Rastrick. James realised that once the faults were ironed out, steam-powered railways would supersede canals completely.However, the climate was not yet ready financially, and even James was heavily committed to completing the proposed canals.

The early 1820s revealed the main drawbacks of waterborne freight transport: a heavy winter could freeze up the boats for weeks on end and a summer drought could leave them high and dry. This vulnerability coupled with the canal owners' refusal to drop the tolls they charged started industrialists looking for an alternative. The time of the railways was at hand.

As the 1820s, progressed a handful of railway ventures were proposed. At first they didn't appear to offer direct competition to the canal system, although William James was pushing for a Grand Central Railway system as early as 1819. The success of the Stockton and Darlington, and even James's Stratford and Moreton, convinced investors of the worth of the new tracks. James had surveyed the Liverpool and Manchester Railway in 1822 and George Stephenson went on to construct it. In 1830 it opened and the railway era had begun.

This picture shows just how well used the canal system was, even though it was in terminal decline at the time the photograph was taken. Each narrow boat holds the same payload as a modern lorry. The maintenance boats on the left have the livery of the Grand Junction Canal Company, one of those that later became the Grand Union. The horse boats passed each other by allowing one horse to stop, letting the tow rope sink, while the other boat was pulled over the sunken rope. It was a delicate manoeuvre requiring a high degree of cooperation.

At the same time as the first locomotives chugged along the railways, photography as we now know it was starting when William Fox Talbot invented a paper film. The silver nitrate-impregnated paper produced a negative image which was fixed by hypo. A second 'contact' print was then taken from this. The resulting picture was a reasonable black and white image, although a trifle grainy. Unfortunately, no images of canals have survived. In France the technology was more complicated. Joseph-Nicephore Niepce and Louis Daguerre went into partnership in 1829. Their process, involving a complicated chemistry on a copper plate, produced a fine-resolution positive image. Both techniques required exposure times of several minutes in strong daylight. The use of silver halides was expensive and photography remained an elite business. Once the cameras were improved by better lenses and a faster photosensitive chemical developed, the Daguerrotype became widely used for portraits and landscape photography.

The railways grew in an almost identical fashion to the canals, a few lonely, risky ventures followed by a wild rush. 'Railway Mania' peaked in 1845 with thousands of miles put before Parliament; like the canals, some would be profitable, some would break even, and some were downright hopeless. With investors throwing money at the railway companies, they started to buy up the canals rather than compete with them. Long-distance heavy freight haulage gradually transferred to rail. The competition between the two became cut-throat, leaving the canal companies with little in the way of profit to invest in their infrastructure, and so once again they became trapped with the working system as it had originally been conceived. It must have been infuriating for the canal companies, but the net result was to start the process whereby the canals have been frozen in time, leaving us with such a treasure.

There was a certain amount of improvement by the more successful companies. The Oxford Canal managed to shorten its overall distance by nearly thirty miles simply by cutting across the winding contour route with cut-and-fill methods, leaving branches and loops that the observant boater can still spot today. The Birmingham Canal Navigation, renowned for its business acumen (normally termed Complete Ruthlessness) from the very beginning, managed to survive and prosper. The BCN, as it is more usually called, had such a network of waterways within the Black Country and Birmingham that the railways had to use it to get their goods to their destinations – it really did reach the parts that others couldn't. A relationship grew up between the BCN and the railway companies that ensured efficient interchange of goods, supply of water, and a thousand other benefits.

On the whole the railways followed the same geographical route that the canals did; easy gradients are essential for both. Very rarely the canal was swallowed up whole by the railway. Normally a railway would plan its route alongside a canal, buy the canal and use it to transport the material to construct the track bed being built nearby. The apparent result was a golden era for the canals but the truth was that the massive cargoes they were carrying were ballast and tracks. The moment the railways were completed, mostly around 1860, trade declined markedly. However, the economy as a whole had grown enormously during the first half of the nineteenth century and Britain had become the most productive industrial nation in the world. America, with its vast natural resources, was only just starting to flex its industrial muscles. Other countries were also eager to modernise, and to do so bought British machinery. The decline in trade was therefore by no means a sudden crash, rather a slow and inexorable loss of market share.

By the late nineteenth century the worlds of photography and canals were beginning to meet. A lower cost method of photograph was unveiled in 1851. Scott Archer's process involved glass plates that had been wetted with a silver halide colloidal coating. The resulting image had a much finer grain than one produced by the Fox Talbot process, but was far more difficult to use since the plates had to be prepared for use just before the exposure. Despite the complications that this produced, the system was so much cheaper that it soon replaced both existing techniques. The exposure time was better, needing only a few seconds, making movement and camera shake less of a problem. Some of the earliest pictures in this book were taken with this technique.

When the railways bought up the canals they did no more than the very minimum maintenance. There were few attempts to modernize the waterways ever again, not that there had been much to start with. No bright, keen managers were anxious to improve productivity – they had all found jobs on the railways. The canals were left to potter along in the way that they had always done. Their working methods, management, even the technology, had been created in the late eighteenth century and there was no impetus, or money, to change any of it. Governments came and went, but the cut continued unaltered.

Photography as we now know it began in 1871 when R.L. Maddox produced a reliable sensitive dry plate. Maddox and others worked on this principle until it was fine-grained and very sensitive, requiring exposures of well under a second. Within a decade George Eastman had developed the roll film and in 1889 the first Kodak camera went on sale. Photography became available to almost everybody, apart from the very poor, of course. The bargees were now very poor indeed since trade had declined so much that many of the larger carrying companies had sold off their boats and turned their backs on the canals.

Many of these company boats were bought by their crews. Usually one family had run the boat for the company, and they now went self-employed. Working on the canal was the only trade they knew, and few of them could read or write enough to get work elsewhere. These owner/drivers, as we would describe them today, called themselves 'Number Ones' after the number of their boat.

The social problems caused by this poverty were twofold. Local villages started to distrust the boat people since they were prone to poaching to supplement their diet and, worse, sometimes brought cholera or flu epidemics out of the cities. Some legislation was passed to ensure that the boats were clean and wholesome to live in and that girls and boys over a certain age didn't have to share a bed. These laws weren't strictly enforced or observed and did little to improve the lot of the average boatman.

The larger canal carrying companies invested in new boats, and especially new engines, towards the end of the nineteenth century. The steam engines that had so successfully powered the railways proved rather too bulky for narrow boats and, needing a crew of four to run, weren't entirely economic. Nevertheless, companies like Fellows Morton and Clayton persisted, and the invention of the diesel engine in 1893 signalled a revolution for canal transport.

Boats, regardless of how antique the canal system is, are an extremely fuel-efficient means of freight transport. The introduction of early diesel engines proved this. A few horsepower of Bolinder engine worked out substantially cheaper to run than a horse and could pull another boat as well. Loads of fifty tons could easily be pulled with a tiny fraction of the fuel used by a train, albeit much more slowly. For heavy freight this wasn't a particular problem and, despite the higher manpower, costs remained competitive. Much of this cost

Braunston High Street. Braunston has always played a central role in the lives of the boatmen and their families.

saving was because the boatmen's pay had remained as frozen as the canal system itself.

In the last century the boatmen and their families had been forced out of their homes and onto their boats. When the canals started they were the kings of the road, so to speak. They could afford to rent houses on the bank, were paid good wages by the companies or entrepreneurs that owned the boats, and frequently had other businesses like pubs or coal merchants. As cargoes disappeared, wages fell and gradually they were forced to either leave the canal life or accept a standard of living far below their fellow workers on the bank. Houses, even furniture, were sold to pay off debts or buy their own boat. Many traditional boats have four brass bed knobs just inside the cabin, a tradition started when that was all that was left from the family home on the bank.

During the 1880s this transition was completed. The narrow canal system had drawn in on itself. As families left the bank and normal society they became reliant on other boaters. Their poverty set them apart and isolated them, leading to the creation of an enclosed society. Literacy was a rare thing and often the canalside families provided the only link between the boaters and the rest of the world. They created a bright and colourful school of art to decorate the tiny, cramped cabins of the boats, often likened to gypsy caravans. Gradually, the world of the bargees and boatmen vanished and as the twentieth century wore on, the brightly painted boats were broken up. For a few years the canals were quiet, reeds growing stealthily across the waters.

The First World War was to prove the crucial turning point in the history of the canal system. It was a labour intensive way of moving goods, not simply in men per tons per boat, but in all the ancillary trades making lock gates, dredging the mud and keeping the hedges trim. After the war there simply weren't enough people left to do all the work. Maintenance schedules were forgotten and many less-used canals started to become unnavigable.

In the 1930s there was a brief flurry of renewed interest. Proposals for a Grand Contour Canal linking all the major ports with a massive inland canal system taking thousand-ton boats were considered … and dropped. A scheme to widen the Grand Union to take fifty-ton barges went ahead but wasn't carried through to a point where it would work easily. For the vast majority of canals the slide into dereliction continued unabated.

There was a resurgence of trade during the Second World War as everything and everyone went to work to defeat fascism. In the aftermath the canals were nationalized along with the railways. Apparently this came as a shock to the government department concerned. The canal system was split from the railways and coupled with the Dockyards to form the Docks and Inland Waterway Executive. The resulting disputes about which union should unload what where did little to enhance the system's reputation. It was then, shortly after the Second World War, that some enlightened people realized that if nothing were done a huge and almost perfectly preserved relic of Britain's industrial heritage would be lost forever. It wasn't just the magnificent achievements of our early civil engineers, the aqueducts and tunnels, vast flights of locks and fascinating architecture, that attracted people to the inland waterways. It was a way of life that had survived unchanged for a century and more. It was the fact you could get on a boat and cruise along them in just the same way as two hundred years earlier.

Although a legacy of fascinating images has been preserved in various archives, the old world of the canals was not widely photographed. At the turn of the century people had little reason to take an interest in this apparently dying transport system. Newer and ever faster trains caught the photographer's eye; the boats were there of course, but taken for granted. Nowadays the sight of a working canal has gone. Holidaymakers laugh and children play on modern boats, but once these waters were the arteries that fed the nation's industry. Cargoes travelled the length and breadth of England day and night.

On the following pages is a selection of glimpses into a world and a way of life that vanished shortly after the First World War. The selection has been drawn from the British Waterways Archive in the main, with a few others where necessary. Some people imagine it as a golden age with the slow plod of horses' hooves along a rustic towpath, but the reality was a busy and hardworking time with deadlines to meet. There was plenty of hard work and little leisure time. The photographs themselves are a testament to the labour and labourers who created the foundations of our modern world.

# 1   Inland waterway boats

The boats on Britain's canals have varied shapes and sizes. The most common, the narrow boat, has evolved from a simple coal carrier into a sleek, efficient craft capable of carrying thirty tons at walking speed pulled by only one horse. At first, most of the boats were owned by large companies such as Pickfords. These large carriers transported parcels and people all across the expanding network, building canalside warehouses at strategic points like Birmingham. The larger collieries and quarries also built and operated huge fleets of boats. In both cases the companies employed their own boatmen. In the early days of the canals these boatmen were well paid masters of the boat. They could afford to rent pleasant houses, often built alongside the new canal. Some canal companies built houses for their boatmen and workers as well as lock-keepers. Thrupp, on the Oxford canal, is an excellent example of this kind of architecture. The census records of the mid-nineteenth century often show that the boatmen and boatbuilders congregated in one part of the town, not far from the cut.

As the railways bloomed, offering cheaper carriage for light parcels and passengers, the larger carrying companies transferred their trade to the rails. They sold off their boats to their crews and more boats became operated by just one family, the famous Number Ones. At first the railways could only compete effectively for light parcel traffic and passengers. Heavy freight like coal remained on the water and the first Number Ones made good money. It wasn't long, however, before the railways could compete for this traffic too and the families found themselves having to find work on the bank or sell up and move on board the boat. As the remaining boat families moved aboard to live, the decoration of each boat became a matter of pride. Paintings of castles appeared on the doorways and highly stylised floral pictures adorned the cabin sides. It is a unique art form that persists strongly on the canals even today.

As railways took the trade from the canals some companies, notably Fellows Morton and Clayton and Cadburys introduced motorised boats. Their first powered boats had huge steam engines and needed a crew of four to operate them. The companies were very proud of their boats, as the photographs show. These steamers were quite rapidly replaced by the first diesel engines around the turn of the century. The early internal combustion engines needed less work to operate and produced more power.

The classic early engine was a Swedish one, the Bolinder. A massive piece of heavy engineering that produced 6hp at first (9hp later), it was a 'semi' diesel, using the heat of the cylinder to vaporize the fuel rather than the injector of modern engines. The single pot had a capacity of around two litres and ran at a couple of hundred revs per minute. You could, and still can, hear the steady thump several miles away. These engines became the industry standard until the invention of the four-stroke diesels by companies like Gardener, Petter and Lister in the 1920s. There are still plenty of original Bolinders thumping away to this day preserving the sound and smell of the early decades of this century in a way that photographs never can.

The result of these motors was the introduction of the 'working pair', an unpowered butty boat towed by a motor boat. It was a system of working that survived until the demise of commercial narrow boat activity. Many of the earlier boats had been operated in pairs on the Grand Union Canal and the working practice became widespread rapidly.

In the north of England some canals were built on a larger scale and used much bigger boats. These craft allowed the introduction of containerization on an industrial scale. The vastly increased loads that the boats could carry, even at the turn of the century, ensured that they could compete with the railways, and in principle means that commercial inland freight transport is still a viable proposition today.

It is sobering to think that, as our motorways become clogged with lorries and our air unfit to breathe from exhaust fumes, a boat is five times more efficient than a train and twenty times more than a lorry. It doesn't go very fast, but then neither does a lorry in a traffic jam!

The sturdy British carthorse. This photograph from the turn of the century shows a horse in its working harness. The boatman too is in his working gear.

All boats had to be pulled by horses until the invention of motors. The first way of doing this was with a pair of donkeys or a single carthorse. As the Victorian era progressed horses were bred to be stronger, culminating in the shire-horse. Most boat horses were not this kind of pedigree, however, but just stout nags. This one is in full harness with all the trimmings, including the little brass ornaments to ward off the evil eye of witches. This is a comparatively recent picture.

The carthorses' placid nature allowed them to be led by even a small child. The dead weight of the boats being hauled along is in excess of seventy tons. As the boats' inertia was substantial, many canals devised ways of helping the horse get the boats going by placing hooks for pulleys so that the towrope could provide a mechanical advantage. Stopping them was another matter altogether, requiring immense skill and timing. This picture appears to be on the Grand Junction Canal near Hillmorton just before the First World War. The Grand Junction Canal became the Grand Union Canal in the 1930s.

A fine pair of horse-drawn boats at the turn of the twentieth century. The whole family was involved in the business of keeping the boats moving. The women are wearing white bonnets, which shows that the photograph was taken before Queen Victoria died – after that they wore black. The leading boat is on the left, and the towed boat (butty) is on the right, with all the various rope guides to ensure the towing rope could be controlled by the butty steerer.

*Opposite*: One horse could pull two boats with up to thirty tons of cargo on each. The leading boat has a fore cabin, a small cabin built in the bows to provide enough accommodation to separate the boys and girls in accordance with the Canal Boats Acts of 1877 and 1884. These Acts were inspired by the Nonconformist George Smith, who campaigned tirelessly for an improvement in the boaters' working conditions. The first Act regulated how much accommodation the people had while the second was supposed to ensure that the children got a proper education. The Acts did at least provide an independent inspection of the boats, which improved conditions somewhat. Only boats owned by large companies had such a luxury as a fore cabin; most families had to survive in the cramped rear cabin.

These small open boats are known as tub boats and were used on the Shrewsbury Canal. A train of them would be pulled by a horse. The advantage of these small boats is that they could be taken into some mines along the drainage channels. The very first English canal, the Bridgewater, took boats right up to the coalface, deep within the heart of a hill. Those boats were 45ft long and 4ft wide and were later called 'starvationers' because they looked as though they had been on a too rigorous diet! These tub boats held about seven tons and could be hauled up and down an inclined plane. The canal itself had been designed to handle these boats rather than narrow boats and was only widened to take standard boats in 1835.

*Opposite*: A brief pause in the day's journey near Tring. It is easy to tell that these boats are tied up from the position of the tiller arm: it is pointing upwards. If a boat is only stationary for a moment the tiller arm is left in its operating position. This practise became a social code. If the arm was down it meant 'We're working, leave us alone.' Up meant, 'Knock on the door and come in for a chat.'

Narrow boats were as common in their day as articulated lorries are today. This pair of Fellows Morton and Clayton boats are just leaving a lock and already the crew of the next boat are preparing to take their vessel through. The Grand Junction Canal was a vital trade artery and constantly busy. The picture dates from 1900.

One of the earliest attempts to use diesel engines was on the Cadburys boat *Bourneville 1*, operating between Bourneville and Knighton. The boat was a great success and convinced many other operators that the future lay not with steam but with the internal combustion engine.

Here *Watford* is being used on a works outing on the North Oxford Canal. This boat had been built in 1879, probably by Mr Farr in Stratford upon Avon where it was registered. Its working life was spent ferrying limestone and cement for the company Greaves Bull and Lakin, who later became the Rugby Cement Company. The picture was taken around 1900.

*Opposite*: The ironically named barge *Tiny*, launched in 1918, was one of several barges built to increase the cargo load on the Grand Junction Canal. The trouble was that they had difficulties passing each other. It was a copy of barges used in the North of England.

No, the baby isn't in charge of the boat; her mum has ducked into the cabin while the boat keeps cruising, her hand still on the tiller while she checks something. The tiller also acts as a handy washing line. With precious little money coming into the family, every moment of every day had to be productive. The boat is a No.1, privately owned.

The introduction of steam engines to the canals was to revolutionize their operation. The engine was bulky and needed three men to operate it, but could run all day and night. The catch was that it took up ten tons of cargo space. The addition of a propeller meant a complete redesign of the stern – the rudder could be smaller but underwater the boat had to be progressively thinner to allow the water to reach the prop.

This Victorian steamer is still afloat and working today. The Fellows Morton and Clayton company was one of the largest canal carrying companies and could afford to invest in these newfangled engines. *Vulcan* had her steam engine replaced by a diesel engine after a while and now sails alongside her sister boat, *President*, who has had her steam engine refitted.

This is a works outing on board a steam-driven inspection launch on the Staffordshire and Worcester Canal. These launches had been the perk of the directors when the canals first opened, but when this picture was taken in 1910 works outings were common and the directors' launch was often commandeered for the job. Unlike the freight-carrying working boats, this one owes much of its design to steam yachts.

Even steamers were vulnerable to stoppages. If a lock broke all the boats were delayed until it was mended. This photograph was taken at Buckby in 1911. The difference between motorboat cabins and those of the horse boats is very clear.

*Opposite*: As the steam boats proved their worth, their design was refined. On the River Weaver they became less like motorized bathtubs and more elegant. The River Weaver navigation dates right back to the days of the South Sea Bubble of the 1720s, long before the era of Canal Mania. As a result it had been built to a broad gauge in order to take riverboats. The navigation was very successful due to the huge mineral and manufacturing trade in the area. It also maintained a process of improvement while many other navigations were stagnating. Between 1840 and 1870 many of the locks were rebuilt or duplicated to increase capacity. The steam tug service enabled boats to get to the docks on the river Mersey. In the 1870s further building enabled the navigation to take 1,000-ton boats, the largest in England until the building of the Manchester Ship Canal.

*Following page*: Steam tugs were used on rivers quite early on. Here, on the River Trent, *Little John* hauls a train of river boats. It seems strange that the tug has such a crude hull design while the keels it is towing have such efficient profiles.

On the huge Aire and Calder navigation steam powered tugs hauled trains of container boats. Their design was detailed and impressive, from their efficient shape down to the unheard of luxury of life belts.

The containers were called 'Tom Puddings' and were used for moving coal. The idea behind them was to simplify the transport of large quantities of coal, either to dockyards for export or to power stations for immediate use. The tugs were able to push or pull the train of containers. If they had to push them, a false bow section was placed at the head of the train. In this picture a false bow has been put in front of the tug, presumably to move it somewhere useful.

Tom Puddings could be lifted onto railway carriages to be taken directly to the power station unloading depot. They were substantially built, as this picture shows.

As the twentieth century wore on the diesel engine was introduced. The smaller size of this type of engine meant a change in the shape of a narrow boat's stern and cabin. The Grand Union Canal Company commisioned Harland and Woolfe to design new narrow boats to use these engines. This picture of a moving pair at Buckby shows just how little wash the new design made.

Inspection launches were used by the canal company directors to check their investment in comfort. It was all a very far cry from the ordinary life of the boatmen.

*Opposite*: Each new diesel-powered boat could pull another unpowered one, the 'Butty'; so the old horse-drawn boats continued to be used. The canals were gradually silting up so that the boats could no longer be loaded to their full capacity, as the butty here shows. This picture was taken near Blisworth on the Grand Union, possibly after the Second World War as the towpath has become very overgrown.

The steamers were the pride of their owners, but they needed a crew of four. This beautiful boat, *Earl*, photographed just after its launch, would not prove to be cost-effective in the long run.

The sad fate of boats that couldn't pay their way. The remains of *Earl* rotted away, abandoned and unwanted.

# 2   Boating folk

The people that worked the narrow boats were not wealthy folk, indeed they lived some of the poorest and hardest lives of any group of workers in late Victorian times. Perhaps the serenity and beauty of the waterways was the only thing that stopped them simply walking away from their boats and working in a factory.

As the impact of the railways on the canal system deepened in the 1860s many large companies sold off their boats to their crews. The 'Number One' was created, one man running his own boat for what ever cargo or route presented itself. At first this was a lucrative job, but as the railways took an ever larger share of the available cargo, loads became scarce and pay dropped. Within twenty years the Number One had frequently had to move his family onto the boat since he couldn't afford a house on the bank. An enclosed, almost secret, society was being formed. The constant travelling meant that the boatman's children couldn't attend school or church. Few of the great philanthropists of the Victorian era ever thought about the boaters and their increasing poverty. Indeed, only a couple of people campaigned for them to be treated more fairly. Society turned its back on the plight of these hard working families, and eventually the boaters turned away from society, creating their own music, art and customs.

Some legislation in the 1870s was designed to prevent the overcrowding of boats; after all, it isn't very healthy to raise seven children in a cabin only ten feet long and six wide. The law wasn't policed very effectively, however. If you examine some of the boats in the pictures you will notice that they have a little cabin at the front – this extra space was supposed to make room for all those children.

By the start of the First World War it had become clear to everyone that something had to be done, and some social work took place. The Boatmen's Institute was founded and provided some education for the children, the Salvation Army converted an old butty into a mission and one famous lady, Sister Mary Ward, ministered to the community's health needs where she could . On the whole though, nothing of any real importance happened until the canals were nationalized after the Second World War, and by then there wasn't much of an industry left to help. Historians refer to objects such as toll tickets and newspapers as 'ephemera', but perhaps the most ephemeral part of the waterways was the lifestyle of the boaters. Today it survives only in the memories of a handful of old people and when they have gone…

Life wasn't too bad if you owned the canal. Here the Directors of the Regents Canal pose for their picture. A finer example of Victorian industrial arrogance you couldn't find.

In contrast, life was unrelentingly hard for most boat people. Endless hard labour on an inadequate diet caused much ill health and suffering. The Number Ones normally had no health insurance or pensions. If the canals froze solid there was no food on the table. If the summer caused a drought the same problems occurred.

A family pauses for their portrait at Braunston in 1909.

Most of the boat women wore large bonnets with a long 'curtain' at the back. They worked outdoors every day and the bonnet was as good as any hat. Their blouses were often heavily embroidered to bulk out the material and make it warmer. A shawl completed the weatherproofing.

*Opposite*: The boatman here is wearing very typical costume: corduroy trousers with a buttoned flap and braces. The flat cap was also very popular. Both men and women wore steel-tipped boots.

This venerable old lady was photographed in a studio. The pose and background look artificial, but the real clue is in the book that she is holding. Hardly any of the Victorian boat people could read or write.

This studio picture of a boat woman shows the typical traditional dress, even if she is startlingly clean! With such cramped accommodation personal cleanliness was something of a luxury.

The young lad in this studio picture looks as though he feels distinctly out of place. The practice of using heavily made corduroy trousers dates right back to the navvies who dug the canals in the first place. Legend has it that their trousers were so strong that they could be left in their will to their sons.

Outside the photographer's studio life was a lot harder. The boat women wore black bonnets to mourn Queen Victoria's death, and kept to that colour afterwards. This photograph was taken in 1922.

Often the only times that the boatmen and their families could meet socially was when a stoppage backed up the boats. In their hectic schedule of deadlines these enforced holidays became a rare chance to catch up on the washing, socializing and courting. Out of a drawer came the Sunday best.

The people working for Fellows Morton and Clayton were better off than the self-employed boaters but, even so, life was hard.

In 1923 the boaters went on strike to protest about their conditions. The FMC depot at Braunston became a focus of the discontent and the police were called out to ensure the law was observed. The boaters' way of life was so scattered across the country that it was a rare sight to see more than a dozen together.

It was probably one of the few times that these boaters were all together at once. This industrial action sadly didn't resolve a great deal and the decline in their standard of living continued. The strike was surprisingly widespread but good-natured. FMC had a very patriarchal attitude towards its staff and on the whole working relations were good.

Back on the cut, the horses were as well fed and dressed as their owners. The cap on the horse is to keep the flies from distracting it and seems better made than the woman's. As with so many archive photographs, there is nothing recorded of the life of the woman staring into the lens – no name, place or date.

Few photographs exist of the boaters' social events. This is a christening at Buckby. It appears to be taking place during a stoppage since the boats are moored right across the canal. It seems to be the only christening ever recorded on film. Presumably the picture dates from after 1901 as the women are wearing black bonnets even at a christening.

*Following page*: Grandma Humphries and her daughter Thirza stop for tea in 1913. The brightly painted Buckby water cans are clearly visible. The boaters even had a favourite type of tea pot. The Measham ware was made near Ashby de la Zouch and became quite a status symbol in the canal world.

The boats were completely without amenities. All the water for drinking and washing was carried in 'Buckby' cans on the cabin roof. Typically, the boaters artwork has spread from the cabin sides onto the water cans. This is Charlie Carter filling them from a public tap.

*Opposite*: For the most part the lives of the boaters went unrecorded by the world around them. Only vague images without even a name survive today.

Washing clothes was impossible on the move; it had to be done on the bank while waiting for a new load. A barrel and a mangle had to suffice right up until the 1960s.

Rose Carter's daughter on one of the Ovaltine boats. The complicated decorative ropework on the rudder is clearly visible.

It didn't matter how big you were, once you were old enough to work, you did. Here Miss Kent pulls the boat in.

Mr Jones and his son Jack astride the donkey. A pair of donkeys could pull as much as one horse and weren't an uncommon sight. Donkeys were much cheaper to buy, required far less in the way of healthcare and could be trained reasonably easily. They still merited some protection from the evil eye by the use of a horse brass.

*Following page*: Mrs Lapworth and her child on board *Cheam*. Babies and toddlers were usually harnessed and tied to the boat so they didn't fall overboard. Clearly visible in this picture, just inside the cabin door, are the bed knobs screwed to the cabin side. This was a long lived tradition: the picture dates from the 1960s.

Boatmen's Institutes were founded in the latter part of the nineteenth century to attempt to better the lot of the boat families. They were mostly at places like Brentford where there was a regularly used dock and provided the only outside source of education and social care available for the boatmen and their families. Only a few vicars paid any attention to the boaters – marriages were informal on the whole and rarely performed in church.

The institute provided regular classes to the children as they passed by Brentford. The children's attendance was dependent on where the cargoes took them, so illiteracy continued. Even the Education Act of 1921 deliberately omitted these children, despite a survey showing that out of the thousand children they found on the canal, only 15% could be called literate.

Although no photographs of weddings survive, here are Jack James's sisters dressed up as bridesmaids.

*Following page*: Domestic life aboard boats in London. Boater's working lives were considerably harder than those of ordinary working men such as those described in Robert Tressel's *The Ragged Trousered Philanthropists*, a book written before the First World War detailing working class life in brutal detail.

The dedication of a school boat. The Bishop and all the local dignitaries attend on one side of the canal while a family of boaters look on from the other. The wide-beam barge had its hold roofed over to make a classroom. The wide barges had not been a great success on the Grand Union canal, so tying one up permanently helped keep the rest of the traffic moving. Quite what the boaters made of all the bigwigs is unrecorded.

One narrow boat was even converted into a floating chapel, but normally the people on the boats were not at all renowned for being religious. The most effective use of these boats was as classrooms and focal points for charities to aid the boatmen.

In Victorian times child labour was considered quite acceptable. These young lads were constructing the Manchester Ship Canal in the 1890s. Their chances of living beyond twenty or thirty were remote in the extreme. There is a modern tendency to view the past with rose coloured spectacles, but the facts show it otherwise.

Boats have always held an appeal for children and often made a marvellous day trip. This crowd are having a fine old time.

This photograph of a school trip was clearly taken before the Health and Safety Executive was created. There's another boatload boarding in the distance. It was taken during the summer of 1914.

A lock-keeper on the River Thames, photographed in 1900. Thames lock-keepers were frequently retired Royal Navy officers and were reputed to keep order in just the same way as they did on ships.

Inside, a narrow boat cabin was cramped but warm and dry. The lace-edged plates hanging on the cabin sides were as popular as Measham teapots. They were threaded with ribbon, the colour of which indicated marital status and suchlike.

An unknown boat woman, looking happy enough with life.

A lock-keeper, probably on a river navigation. Many archive pictures survive with no information about them apart from a brief title.

When a boatman died his coffin would be carried to his final resting place on a boat bedecked with ivy and wild flowers.

The boat would have all the locks set ready for it and boat people would gather to give him a final farewell. As with the photographs of the christening earlier, these are the only photographs that exist. The boaters lived in such an enclosed world that by the time photography became commonplace, few outsiders with cameras were welcomed. The boaters couldn't afford enough food let alone their own cameras. Funerals were common enough, but not often photographed.

# 3   Working boats

The sight of a gaily painted pair of boats cruising along a canal has always appealed to people. As a result, boats have been photographed at work for as long as cameras have been portable enough to take to the canal. The very earliest portable cameras were quite a handful, needing a tripod to take their weight. Film speeds were often so slow that the subject had to remain motionless for several seconds. As photographic technology improved, cameras became lighter and film speeds faster. Early plastics replaced the glass negatives and as the twentieth century wore on action shots became possible.

The slow speed of the earliest photographs produces some interesting effects. Although the photographer could ask people to stay still, water is never stationary, and the ripples present during the exposure produce a strange, misty appearance to the canal. Another thing to look out for is the person who moved - there's almost always someone who coughed or twitched, despite the earnest entreaties of the photographer. They are the blurred one!

Working a boat was undeniably hard. The cargo had to be moved whatever the weather, indeed in the winter the demand for coal was at its height. We are lucky enough to have pictures of a horse-drawn ice-breaker in action. Pulled by a team of horses, the boat was rocked from side to side so that it rode up over the ice and then smashed down to open a channel. The boat photographed looks as though it was nearly rocked right over! It was a dangerous job.

Legging boats through tunnels was another hazardous occupation. Only a few of the tunnels have towpaths; for the rest it was a matter of a couple of men lying on a plank across the boat and walking it through. Some of the tunnels are over a mile long and the journey could take a couple of hours. Not surprisingly some of the first motorized boats were tunnel tugs, but even that was dangerous – the fumes from the steam engine could suffocate the crews.

Most of the work was simply plodding along behind the horse and waiting patiently for the locks to fill, loading sacks or shovelling coal. It was a pace of life that can still be experienced on the canals, but at least you don't have to unload thirty tons of nutty slack at the end of a cruise today!

Here a narrow boat is being loaded with containers from a horse-drawn plateway at Little Eaton. This sight was rare even in 1900 when the picture was taken. The fascinating feature of this photograph is the use of containers. The boxes were craned onto the boat from small four-wheeled waggons. Tramways and plateways (a plateway is a railed track with the flanges on the rail rather than the vehicle wheel) were frequently constructed to bring heavy goods from a mine or quarry to a nearby canal. They were in use from the very start of the canal era and formed the inspiration for the railway system. Strangely enough, the use of containers was fairly restricted despite the fact that it made loading boats so much quicker.

*Opposite*: Thomas Clayton was a famous canal carrier specialising in the transport of coal tar from gas works. The coal tar was a cargo that neither the railways or roads wanted, so the traffic on the canals lasted virtually up until the introduction of natural gas. Mrs Smith and her daughter (and the dog) are on board the boat *Gifford*. The boat can sometimes be seen at the Black Country Museum.

Steering a motorboat or butty was hard work, especially on tight bends when both boats had to pivot about their centres. It required a consummate degree of skill, timing and strength to avoid the momentum of the boat ramming it into the bank.

Clayton's boats were mostly horse-drawn. Ben Smith and his horse walked many a long mile of towpath.

A pair of horse boats passing through Buckby Locks at the turn of the century. The babies used to be tied to a tether on the roof to stop them crawling too far and over the edge!

This pair of unladen boats is caught having a brief rest by the camera. The photograph was originally taken on a glass plate, which broke. Hence the two fracture marks on the right of the frame. Although the wet plate process was not as accurate as the earlier daguerreotype, the exposure speed was fast enough to catch a wealth of detail.

Another pair of boats at Buckby. It was a popular spot for photographers as well as boats.

This boat was one of the early experiments in using internal combustion engines. Cadbury's chocolate manufacturers were another pioneer of the diesel engine. This craft was launched in 1906. The introduction of the diesel was to improve the economics of canal transport immensely, unfortunately too late to save much of the canal system from decline.

This is an ice-breaker boat, photographed in 1895 at Great Lindford. These boats were essential to break a channel through the ice in winter. Constructed with massive oak timbers and clad in iron plates, the boats used main force to ride up onto the ice and smash down through it. The men clung onto a central rail and rocked the boat to widen the broken channel for the boats behind.

This ice-boat is being hauled by a team of several heavy horses and rocked vigorously from side to side.

So vigorously, indeed, that the boat appears to be in danger of completely capsizing.

The moment the channel was free of ice, boats would pour down it, working through the night sometimes, so that the ice didn't have a chance to reform and lock in the boats again.

*Opposite top*: Strong iron boats could withstand the ice better than wooden ones. This one, *Penguin*, seems quite at home in it! The introduction of two-cylinder, four-stroke diesels in the 1930s gave the motorboats a huge increase in power, enabling them to break their own ice and pull several butties at the same time.

*Opposite bottom*: It wasn't often that the boats were stationary long enough for one to realize how many of them there really were. This is just a small part of the Grand Union Canal Carrying Company fleet tied up in London. In the decades after the First World War smaller canals and carrying companies started to amalgamate to form comapnies like the GUCCC. A huge, partly government funded, improvement programme was carried out to improve the backbone of the canal system, the London to Birmingham route.

The Fellows Morton and Clayton fleet was nearly as large and maintained its independence until after nationalization.

Outside the industrial cities the canals maintained their rural charm. Here at Aynho in Oxfordshire, a boat unloads its cargo of coal. The scene is not that different today except that the boats are holiday hire craft.

Joe Buckler's boat *Joseph Ernest*.

A quiet scene at Nashmills. The boat is clearly tied up and stopped, the whole scene posed for the camera.

A diesel motorboat towing a butty, heavily laden with coal for the Ovaltine works.

*Opposite*: When a lock closed, a traffic jam built up very quickly. Here at Cowroast locks near Tring it looks as though they've been there long enough to set up a floating town. Such events weren't uncommon, and although they allowed the boaters to have some social life, it meant that they were not being paid.

Loading boats on a canal is a lot easier than on a river. Here on the river Trent a trailer has been lowered into the water beside the boat since it cannot reach the side. No doubt the traction engine is there to pull it out again.

Another stoppage, this time in 1906. All four of the Fellows Morton and Clayton steamers are sitting around idle. Stoppages like this proved expensive for the canal carriers.

A line of boats near the south end of Braunston Tunnel. A tunnel tug blows off steam just behind a launch on the off side.

A fairly typical scene on the Grand Junction Canal at the turn of the century. Until this time the vast majority of boats were horse-drawn. This meant that the effort to move the boats, the drag of the horses hooves, was applied to the towpath. The water in the canal remained comparatively still and there was a very low level of bank erosion. This meant that the canal companies did not need a huge dredging programme. Repairing the towpath was simple enough. With the advent of motorized boats the motivating force moved from the towpath to the water and bank erosion increased dramatically.

Narrow boats carried virtually any cargo. Here a boat is being loaded with the harvest of a field near Maids Moreton in around 1900.

Reeds were a very useful commodity, being used for rush lights and thatching houses. In 1880, when this picture was taken, there was a large trade in reeds to London. Although there were paraffin lamps and candles, many poor people had to make do with rush lights.

*Opposite*: This boat, just visible beneath its load, is loading grass cut from the towpath. Canals with horse-drawn boats are a very 'green' transport system; even the grass on the banks is the fuel for the horses.

Peaceful cruising on the Grand Union Canal.

# 4   Canal accidents

If there's one thing that has always attracted a crowd (and the photographers), it's an accident. Luckily the low speeds of canal boats don't create the kind of carnage that car crashes do. Boats have always bumped into each other but the usual result was a lot of bad language and perhaps a sprung plank. There were plenty of working practices that led to embarrassing situations, however.

Boats earned their money by carrying as much cargo as they could. The trouble for a boat is that if you overload it, it sinks! When a boat was first launched it was 'gauged' – the canal companies charged tolls on the tonnage carried and so measured the capacity of a boat by loading one ton blocks into it and recording how much the boat sank down. On the old gauging records there is a list of measurements of the inches showing above the water for each ton block loaded. The boat would start empty and the measurement would be forty inches or so, and the last entry would be something like '38 tons, 1/2 inch'. In other words, there was only a half-inch of the boat above the water – it would only take the ripple from another boat to lose that… and down she went! The trouble was that the boats weren't simply cargo carriers. The little cabin was a whole family's home. Periodically boats were re-gauged, particularly if they had been refitted. It was then that an established family home could find itself at the bottom of the cut.

Some disasters were more spectacular. When a canal embankment broke, thousands of tons of water and mud would flood out and sometimes any boats unlucky enough to be on that water went with it. The most dramatic of all disasters took place on 2 October 1874. It was a salutary lesson about mixed cargoes; petrol, oil and gunpowder are not a good mix. Macclesfield Bridge was known afterwards (following rebuilding) as 'Blow Up Bridge'. The cost to the canal company was so great that they gave up carrying altogether.

Because the cabin at the back of a boat was empty, many coal boats stacked the coal higher just in front of it to weigh the stern of the boat down. They even used boards to get that little bit of extra weight on. But a bit too much could have dire results like this…

…or this. The Fellows Morton and Clayton butty *Orange* shows how deep the canal is. Someone was going to be in a lot of trouble.

When the boats were gauged in the weigh dock, they were loaded to their theoretical maximum, with less than ten millimetres of boat showing over the water. It only takes a little ripple to flood the boat at that point. This FMC josher demonstrates the fact graphically. Brentford weighing dock managed to sink a few boats in 1910.

When the boat is also your home an accident in the weigh dock, or anywhere else, is a disaster. It's hardly surprising that this family look gloomy. There were a lot of children to sleep in only the one cabin that night. Clothes, food, all their possessions were ruined, at a time when there no state help apart from the workhouse.

Tidal stretches of canals and rivers have many dangers. Hidden currents can whisk a boat out of control, leaving one end stuck on a wharf while the other drops with the tide. Here at Brentford on the tidal Thames a boat has come to grief in just this manner.

Even stout masonry aqueducts could collapse. This one at Barnsley gave way in most spectacular fashion on 30 November 1911.

*Opposite*: Canals are very sturdy structures, but they have their weak points. Embankments are particularly prone to leaking and sometimes bursting. After a prolonged spell of heavy rain the sides weaken and the pressure of the water in the canal can cause them to burst open. The resulting flood of escaping water can carry boats along with it and spill them out of the canal. This burst was at Northwich in 1907.

This burst at Brentford shows the power of the water to scour away soil and walls along its path. An accident like this would close the canals for weeks, or even months and freight had to be routed another way. Often the trade never returned and the demise of the commercial waterway system accelerated.

*Opposite*: It may be difficult to see from this photograph, but before 1874 there was a lovely ornate canal bridge here. A boat laden with flammable goods and gunpowder exploded beneath it and from then on Macclesfield Bridge was known as 'Blow Up Bridge'. The boat, *Tilbury*, had around five tons of gunpowder and three barrels of petrol on board and was the fifth boat in a train of six. The first was a steam tug, *The Ready*, prone to issuing showers of sparks from her funnel. At the point of explosion, most of the train had passed under the bridge at the northern end of the Regents Canal. The blast completely destroyed the boat and bridge, sank one of the other boats and killed several people including the crew. Windows were blown in for half a mile around and the bang was heard twelve miles away.

The burst of the Bolton and Bury Canal nearly carried this container boat right down a hillside. The local railways usually took over the paralysed freight trade.

A second look at the Northwich canal burst of 1907, showing how deep the hole scoured by the escaping water is – deep enough to hold one boat on top of another. The one further away had a lucky escape. Water may look placid, but it has an awesome power.

From an historical perspective, the most dangerous thing for the canals was neglect. As early as 1913 some canals like the Basingstoke here were becoming derelict through lack of traffic. The constant movement of boats was important to keep the weeds under control.

One last attempt to navigate the difficult canal was made by the boat *Basingstoke* and its skipper A.J. Harmsworth. Without regular boat traffic the weeds were reclaiming the cut.

The attempt failed. The weeds had choked the life out of the canal and the navigation was lost. The wildlife dependant on the clear, open water moved elsewhere and for the next seventy years the canal became a stagnant liability. The story has a happy ending though: today the Basingstoke canal has been substantially restored and boats once again ply its waters. The wildlife is starting to return and the future looks brighter all round.

# 5  Canal features

Canals are remarkably simple. Most of the system is simply a clay-lined ditch full of water. The early canal builders soon had to contend with hills, and locks were built to raise and lower the boats between different heights of water. Individually, a lock is not that impressive, but when grouped into flights to ascend a steep hill, they can become quite a feature in the landscape. Each canal company designed its canal with a unique architecture, from the materials for the walls and lock gates to all the details like houses and docks. At first much of the canals' equipment was made of wood, cheap and quick to make. The original lock equipment soon wore out though and was replaced in the main with cast-iron fittings. Buildings are more durable and many warehouses, bridges and locks remain in their original condition. They form a priceless heritage.

Later generations of civil engineers tried to overcome the cost and time that working a boat up a flight of locks cost by making boat lifts. The Foxton Inclined Plane was one such attempt, although it was only in use for a few decades. The decline in traffic meant that it was too expensive to use and it was demolished. The best known surviving lift is the Anderton Lift. It looks much the same today as it did when it was built, despite conversion to electricity and other alterations. Beneath the paintwork the metal structure has been badly affected by corrosion and it will require a massive effort to re-open it.

Tunnels were an alternative to huge lock flights too. Why go over a hill when you could go right through it? At the end of the eighteenth century tunnels were dug by hand. With pickaxes, shovels and the occasional handful of gunpowder, the navvies bored through hills of solid rock. The tunnels sometimes took decades to complete, but most of them have lasted intact to this day. Tunnels sometimes provided extra income for the canal company when they passed through seams of coal or limestone: side tunnels were driven into these deposits to extract the minerals. Dudley Tunnel, in the Black Country Museum, provides the visitor with a unique chance to experience the maze of underground waterways that were the result of this serendipity.

Tunnels were always a bottleneck in the system, however, and if it was possible to avoid them the surveyors would do so. The risk involved in driving a tunnel was substantial. The Leominster Canal experienced so much trouble with its tunnels that it was never completed. The surveyor Thomas Dadford recommended four tunnels. One of the three that were built, Southnet Tunnel, collapsed on the workers who were finishing it. The accident claimed the lives of the foreman and four labourers and was the final straw for the company, who lost interest in a project that had been overambitious from the start. Most tunnels claimed their toll on the workers lives, sometimes as many as one for each yard driven.

Other tunnels suffered from subsidence. Harecastle Tunnel began to settle and a new one was built beside it. Today the bore has settled so low that it is completely unnavigable. Lappal Tunnel in Birmingham is another to suffer the same fate.

Docks are always interesting places. The canals had their own set of wharves in the most unlikely places. Today almost all trace of them has gone, but you can find the odd clue to their existence in the street names of a town. A 'Wharf Street' is often all that is left, while the canal basin site has been turned into a bus station or car park. Famous towns like Stratford-on-Avon and Oxford had their own docklands, but you would scarcely believe it today. The smaller details of canal architecture such as paddle starts and small accommodation bridges have suffered badly over the years. Many of these smaller features have been replaced with mass-produced iron items common to all canals in England. Canals that are being brought back into use now tend to be fitted with modern equipment rather than their own unique gear.

One of the largest lock flights in Britain is on the Grand Union at Hatton, near Warwick. Today it comprises of wide locks and is a popular spot to watch boats at work. At the turn of the century the original narrow locks were in use. The flight was known as 'The Stairway to Heaven'.

The top of a flight of locks was always a special place. Canal offices and wharves were often built here. This is Stoke Bruerne a century ago. It is now a waterways museum.

Cassiobury Park Lock, Watford. On the left is a typical canal cottage, rather small and built on a tight budget to house the lock-keeper.

Canal basins in cities were busy centres of trade. Here, at Paddington, London, goods arrived from all over the country and cargoes from ships were carried back to the provinces. This picture from 1909 shows the variety of horse-drawn boats that were in service.

*Previous page*: Narrow boats continued to work after the Second World War. Here a group of boats are waiting for loads on the Thames. They are painted in the dull blue and yellow colours of British Waterways, the body that emerged after the canals were nationalized.

Sharpness, on the Severn Estuary, became a major port in the nineteenth century. Here ships from all over the world wait to transfer their cargoes into barges capable of working the canals and rivers. In 1890 Britain was one of the worlds largest economies and our overseas trade was enormous. The Gloucester and Sharpness Canal was one of the last to be opened at the start of the nineteenth century. It was designed to bypass the treacherous section of the Severn Estuary leading into Gloucester and was a ship canal in conception, built on a scale to suit international freighters.

Sharpness never became renowned as a naval port because of the dangerous waters of the estuary, but from here goods could be transferred into narrow boats for quick transit to the Midlands. This photograph was taken just before the First World War.

Gloucester, at the other end of the ship canal, was an inland port of some significance. Smaller ships could navigate to the docks and in 1911 a wide assortment of boats could be found here.

Coal and canals are inextricably linked, especially in the Black Country. The canal system was born out of the need to transport coal and here at Hednesford the number of boats needed to do the job is graphically illustrated. The boats are known as 'Joeys', after Joseph Chamberlain, the Mayor of Birmingham. Their journeys were almost always completed within a day, so the cabins, if they were fitted at all, were very modest, small affairs quite unlike those of the long-distance boats. Joeys were frequently made double-ended so that to reverse direction the rudder was simply lifted off one end and stuck on the other. Coalfields and quarries were the principal source of cargoes for the canal system at first, although little remains of them these days.

*Opposite*: Regents Dock, London, another scene of feverish activity. Britain's industry required vast quantities of imported raw materials and was exporting machinery to all corners of the globe.

The coal was destined for power stations and furnaces around the Midlands. Here at Nechells Power Station boats wait to be unloaded before returning to the colliery. Despite the massive change to rail transport, in the Black Country the existing network of canals and collieries remained a cost-effective transport system. A new type of Joey boat was designed for use solely on this part of the canal. The 'Hampton boat' (short for Wolverhampton) was 8ft wide and 80ft long. Capable of carrying nearly fifty tons, it ensured the continuation of the coal trade until subsidence closed the canal in the 1960s.

The power stations needed an unending supply of coal. Walsall Power Station installed mechanical grabs to speed up unloading. The boats got battered about in the process, but then they were cheap enough to replace quickly. Norton Canes boat yard was reputed to build them by the mile and cut off what was needed.

Oxford might have a refined and intellectual reputation but the residents still needed their coal. It was unloaded at a basin in the city centre. The site is now a bus station.

The Fellows Morton and Clayton company built their own depots and had a fleet of lorries to distribute the cargoes around a city. One or two boatmen were taught to drive lorries but since they weren't used to using brakes it wasn't always successful.

Ellesmere Port was another massive dock complex. Today it houses a waterways museum and preserved historic boats.

The River Thames has always been a busy waterwa, and never more so than at the turn of the twentieth century.

Foxton Inclined Plane was created to speed boats past a bottleneck of locks. It consisted of two tanks rolling on rail tracks up and down the hill. The boats floated into the tanks, the doors were closed and the boats and water rolled to the next level. The construction took several years and the lift opened in 1900.

Although the tanks were designed to counterbalance each other, a huge steam winch was needed to overcome the friction.

*Opposite top*: Foxton Inclined Plane carried boats past the locks for only a few decades and was then broken up for scrap. The site is still an interesting place to visit. The locks are still there, and still a bottleneck. A charity exists to preserve what remains.

*Opposite bottom*: Anderton Boat Lift, in Cheshire, lifts boats vertically. Originally the two tanks were balanced and, by letting a little water out of the one at the bottom, the top one would descend, lifting the other as it did. Eventually the two tanks were operated separately by electricity. The iron structure has suffered substantial corrosion from the salty air but it is being restored.

The Oxford Canal had a tunnel built on its summit level. It was such a nuisance that eventually the canal company took the dramatic step of removing the soil above it and opening it out. If you cruise this section of canal today you can still catch a glimpse of the original brick tunnel lining. This is one of the earliest canal photographs in existence, taken in 1869.

Blisworth tunnel took years to build and needed constant maintenance ever afterwards. This picture is of the local work force on a maintenance boat, with a tunnel tug behind them.

Harecastle Tunnel is one of the longest canal tunnels ever built. This is the new tunnel, while on the right is the entrance to the old tunnel.

Above ground there is little sign of the tunnel below. Here a winch is placed above an access shaft to lower building materials to the workmen below.

Working deep underground in a canal tunnel was just as dangerous as in any coal mine. This photograph shows the workforce inside Blisworth in 1910.

After tunnels and power stations, a pleasant scene on the Llangollen Canal in rural Wales. Even here you can be sure there will be a tramcart full of something to load onto the boat any minute.

# 6   Working the canals

The canal system was a huge concern, more or less the same size as today's motorway system. It had to be maintained by thousands of workman, some highly skilled. There were carpenters for making the lock gates, lengthsmen to inspect each yard of the waterway, lock-keepers and toll collectors. Although the colourful lives of the boat families often capture the imagination, supporting their way of life was an army of workers keeping the canals in working order.

As the nineteenth century came to an end, the railway companies cut back on their canal maintenance duties. Later the fearful loss of life in the First World War reduced the workforce available even if the will to regenerate the canals had existed. The decline of the waterways system stemmed in part from the lack of sufficient people to carry out the labour-intensive work of keeping the canals open.

The work wasn't solely wading around up to the knees in mud, cleaning a canal. There were boats to be built too. Boat-building techniques were the same on the inland waterways as for seagoing boats. The design was different but the traditional tools and crafts had been handed down through the generations from time immemorial. Boats were normally made of wood, usually with an elm bottom and oak sides. The planks were placed in a steam jacket to soften them enough to be curved into the fine lines at the boats bow and stern.

Iron boats had been used on the canals from very early on, but their cost was high and it wasn't until the twentieth century that they became a common sight. A wooden boat could be made in a week or so, cost a few hundred pounds and last twenty-five years or more. An iron boat cost three or four times that but could last fifty before needing major repairs. Today there are only a handful of wooden boats left but there are plenty of enthusiasts who own original iron working boats over a hundred years old and still carrying cargoes.

Canals have always suffered from silting. Eventually the canal would become too shallow for the boats to pass and the remedy was to shovel the mud out. Here at Deanshanger in 1902 a gang of workers set to with a will. When the canals used only horses for traction the silting was comparatively slow. The introduction of propeller driven boats accelerated the process of bank erosion and silting dramatically.

*Opposite top*: This gang in 1910 are using long planks to allow barrows to remove the mud from the cut.

*Opposite bottom*: Each canal company had workshops to make lock gates. The gates took a lot of punishment in use. Forty tons of boat without brakes can easily smash them and so there was a constant need for new ones. Most gates were made of oak that came from trees felled during the winter. This practice ensure the grain of the wood was tight and free of sap. Usually the wood was worked before seasoning since it became too hard as it aged.

*Pages 120-121*: The gates had to be fitted with such precision that they were watertight. A gate like this weighs nearly two tons, and in 1900 only the most basic lifting equipment was available.

Before the First World War there was no shortage of labour, although the rates of pay for this dirty and backbreaking work were very low. After the war work such as this was rarely carried out.

The Grand Junction Canal was widened in the 1930s to allow larger boats to use it. Here at Braunston the work is in progress. Much of the canal between London and Birmingham was repaired, widened and strengthened.

Every now and then a lock would have to be completely rebuilt. The weight of water in the ground around a lock can crush it. The only solution is to renew the walls. The canal companies employed plenty of bricklayers to make the repairs as quick as possible.

This picture illustrates clearly how a bridge arch is formed on a wooden former. Once the arch is complete it can take many tons of road and vehicles on top of it. It's a pity the womans dress obscures the detail on the keystone.

In 1910 Starveall Bridge developed some serious cracks, visible on the right-hand walls. These are the emergency repairs and shoring that were needed.

The staff of a typical boatbuilder's yard. Two of the men are holding tools that look rather like an axe but with a flat blade. This is known as an adze and has been used to make wooden boats since medieval times.

Bushells boat yard in 1894. The boats were usually made in a row. The boat under construction shows clearly the length of the keelson along the bottom of the hull, the stem post and the start of the planking. Narrow boats are normally launched sideways into the water.

The same yard in 1919.

A typical small boat builder's yard. This is at Tusses Bridge, Hawkesbury, near Coventry.

Fellows Morton and Clayton, being one of the largest canal carriers, naturally had one of the largest docks. Here at Saltley in 1897 they are repairing and building boats to keep the huge fleet going.

Walkers Boatyard. The boat *Stentor* shows the way the stern of a motorboat looks. The large, slow-revving propeller is beneath the stern deck and the sides of the boat have been brought in to allow the water to reach the prop.

This picture shows the way that the oak planks are shaped and joined to the stem post at the bows of the boat. This type of construction has remained the same throughout the entire history of the canal system.

To make a wooden boat requires strength – and a big hammer! Here at Peter Keays boatyard one of the last wooden boats to be built takes shape.

With the simplest of traditional tools, a wooden boat can be made well enough to last in commercial use for thirty years. It can carry the same load as an articulated lorry for that time, and while it is working more trees can be grown to build its replacement. The boat needs a twentieth of the fuel to operate and is, when all is said and done, far more environmentally acceptable.